A Garage Sale of Lovelorn Things

SHRUTEE CHOUDHARY

First published in 2021 by

Becomeshakespeare.com

One Point Six Technologies Pvt Ltd.
119-123, 1st Floor, Building J2, B - Wing,
WadalaTruck Terminal, Wadala East, Mumbai,
Maharashtra, India, 400022.
T: +91 8080226699

ISBN - 978-93-5438-351-9

About the author:

Shrutee Choudhary is an actor and a writer, based in Mumbai. She began writing as a child, in attempts to mimic the worlds she so often escaped into through various books. The poet in her, however, quite naturally leapt out as a teenager, and she has found an outlet through words ever since. She loves to tell stories, whether it is through her performance, travel or writing.

She has a mass following on Instagram. Follow her work on @shruteechoudhary

Acknowledgement:

I'm grateful to my parents for showing constant faith and support, my friends for the same, if not more. For the periodic push that I terribly needed in order to stop procrastinating; Prachi Mehta, for illustrating my little book and giving my poems a visual semblance; and last but not the least, my pets, Simba and Kelsey, simply for existing.

Foreword:

The title of this book came to me with a poem, as an instantaneous feeling that never quite left me. I have been holding on to it for several years now, in the hopes of publishing my collection of poetry by the same name. The idea behind the book is simple. It's metaphorical in the truest sense, as you will find, when you continue to flip through the pages.

More often than not, we tend to assign value to objects, especially during difficult times. They become so much more to us than their innate purpose. They are no longer mere things, they are reveries, an ache for lost times, a remembrance. We hold onto them because the alternative is so much harder. Letting go means never being able to escape to those lost realms again. But it is essential, in order to move on.

As you read the poems, you will find that they are not arranged in any order, much like the process of moving on, this book isn't linear. Rather, it's a mishmash of emotions, scattered, messy, much like the unused objects that we tend to hold onto, longer than usual.

With this, I hope we can take on an inward journey, and declutter our hearts and minds of whatever weighs on us and pulls us down. All those heartbreaks and traumatic events that have been holding us back, let us

put them in boxes, not to store in a dingy, dark corner;
but to get rid of, permanently…

In a garage sale of lovelorn things!

1.

I remember ceaseless conversations
stolen glances and mixtapes, and realising how
nothingness could mean everything, sometimes.
I remember your scent on my skin, my favourite perfume
my lipstick-stained mouth feeling yours break into a smile.
I remember your hand in my hand — my heart in yours.
I remember your body thrown over mine, like the warmest
blanket on a shivery night. I remember knowing an
unfounded, paralysing
kind of fear gnawing on my insides. The fear of to being
with you tomorrow
or at all. I remember finally being able to comprehend
why people wish to freeze time.

The sky was the spectator that night while we lay counting
stars
In the galaxies of our eyes, and I remember thinking
If at all magic existed, that this was it — you and I
together, living an eternal summer.

2.

I am wide awake in the aftertaste of
midnight
my mind is a meteor shower
my heart, once a dying ember is now
a wildfire

I close my eyes
I see us
walking aimlessly, hand in hand
unaware of our whereabouts
maybe it was written in the stars

I open my eyes
to the sound of my breath
I think of the feeling
you envelope me in
so often

everything I am so afraid of
seems inconsequential
in your
proximity

I turn to the empty half of the bed
my hands retrace
the vague imprint of your face
on the
pillow

your face
the sight of which is like the Sun rising
so familiar and yet

just as mesmerising
each time

I ache to be with you
and not just now

I ache to spend
year after year
In your nearness

sleepless
I stir with revelations
fearless
I let them unfold

because love is no longer a word
It is a composite of us

and I'm no longer myself, without you.

rain

3.

I met you for the first time with a sense of nostalgia.
Maybe I had known you in another time another
life.

your scent came to me in whiffs, like the smell of rain
from last year and like the raw breeze I felt you
on my bare skin. It was as if I had held those very hands
kissed those very lips, been in those very arms
and with every touch I was closer to where I belong

as if I was a drifter, finally returning home

such a strange feeling it is to meet someone for the first time
And reminisce a life you are yet to spend together

maybe it is an aftermath of alchemy that happens to all
star crossed lovers or maybe
It is a rare phenomenon that happened to the two of us

but it is as if I had loved you long before I even met you
and I know I will love you, all over again.

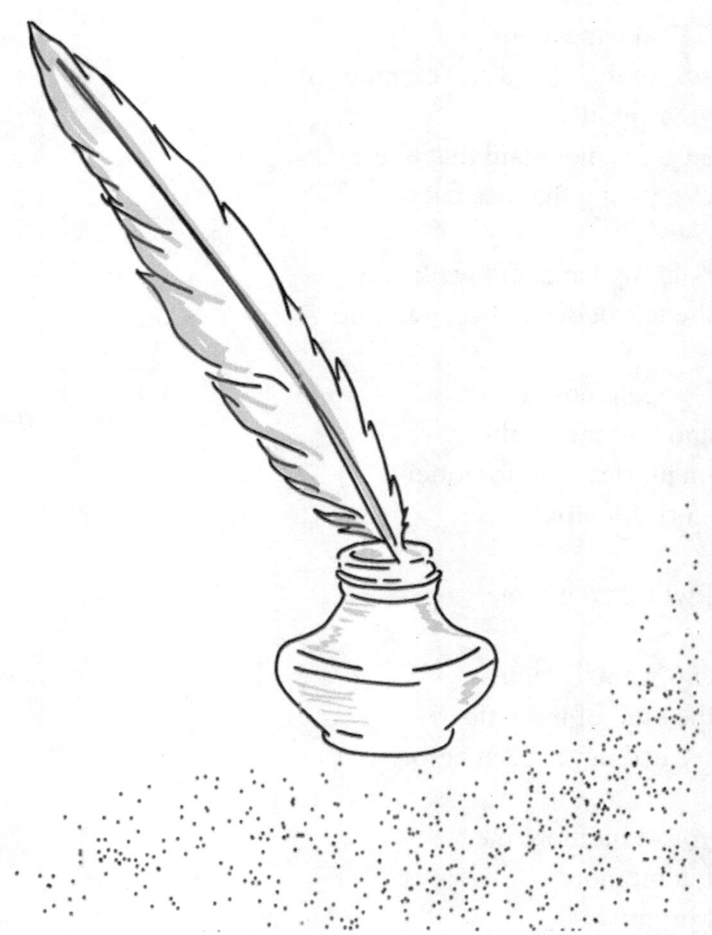

4.

Take me along
to the nooks and crannies of
your mind
atop the mountain that overlooks
everything that has been

hold my hand and walk along
the untrodden alleys, unafraid

let open those doors
and that they hold
memories long forgotten
stories, untold

I will do the same

and we will return
the kind of intimate
we had never been before

you, a bit more me
I, a bit more you
I promise.

5.

That is how I felt when you left
like two pages glued together for too long
had vehemently been uncoupled

our story once penned in indelible ink
was now barely decipherable

we were like paragraphs torn into phrases
that made no sense on their own

you walked away
relentlessly so

and I watched you take along
pieces of me, that wouldn't let go.

6.

Like the hills
frozen in time
cold and veiled
by the night
there I was

awaiting
the morning sun
Its unearthly light
to kiss the brink
of my soul

there you were
bringing me back to life.

7.

The night your heart breaks. When you fall asleep because your swollen eyes can't cry anymore. the sleep, which you cling onto with clenched fists and your fingers digging into your skin. It hurts but it also feels so safe. You're away from reality and how.

The morning that follows.

For a split second, you're not scarred. For a fleeting moment, it feels like a vague nightmare. For a minute, you are relieved. You actually believe that is all that it was - your worst fears playing with your mind. And then it hits you, with a greater intensity as you realise that even the humble morning sunlight cannot take away the perpetual murk of a broken heart.

Once again your heart aches and you disintegrate within no time.

8.

I peeked into your soul and saw nothing, just miles and miles of darkness
that could engulf even the brightest star. The inky blackness
of your eyes called out to me and suddenly, I found myself
wanting to free-fall into perpetual nighttime, to call this void my home.

Daylight meant nothing, as long as I was somehow, yours.

9.

Loving you
was indelicate and restless
It was wild and desperate
colossal and reckless
It was an unquenchable thirst
for every inch of you on me
filling all my voids
a catastrophic collision
of your presence
with all my hours
Loving you
was like loving
the waves that come
only to leave again
I had to devour you whole
In the little time we had

10.

We walked that day with no purpose. we didn't
know where we were going or what we were
doing. It was a beautiful day, I had you next to me and
that was enough.

we walked the same streets, we saw the same things.
when silence fell, we could still speak.. our souls could
interact. I don't think you ever existed the way you did
to me, that day. there was enough space between us, yet
we were so intimate. the kind that goes by unnoticed
most of the time. but I felt it, I felt it on every inch
of my yearning skin, in every piece of my dismantled
heart. after all this time, I still do. It is the only thing I
want to hold onto.

11.

Here you are
next to me
waiting to disappear
I can already feel you go
So kiss me under the sun
and in darkness
at places only we know
So I never forget
why it's important to me
to be next to you

12.

I look up to see your face against the sky
like that one white cloud on a perfect summer day
you talk of bright futures
you tell me you will stay
I know you will vanish
If not today
then someday
like that one white cloud on a perfect summer day
I can already see you go
I'll remember you though
In pieces
the tiny fragments
In your fabric
that makes you
I'll remember you like that
until you're blended
with me in a way
I can't tell us apart

13.

All my eyes could see
all there ever was
amidst miles of mist
and looming darkness
was a storm brewing
out of a kiss, here
and a kiss, there
and out of hands clasped together
ever so tightly
that your flesh
was my flesh
and my heart
was yours
and the raindrops
curtained our window sill
only my heartbeat danced
to the rhythm of your breath
everything else had come to a standstill
as you consumed
my time

and the rest of me
little by little
I swear
my monochrome reality
was painted in your colour

and we drove past
tall trees
on mountain roads
In a raging thunderstorm
chaotic and breathtaking and transitory
and in those fleeting minutes
I knew
You did to me
what any storm would do to a place
You wreaked havoc
then left me
devastatingly beautiful
In your aftertaste

14.

It's after 2 at night and it's awfully quiet, everywhere but in my head. I have a lot of things to say -- some are words of hate, some of anger, the rest are just jumbled attempts of telling you I want to fix this. But how can I just call you and resolve it, after what you did? I wanted to say sorry, a second before what happened. Then I just couldn't. I still can't. I'm furious. I can't forgive this. You. I love you. But.

It's easy when I'm not around you. I usually get distracted by the complexities and anxieties that my days have to offer. It's only after 2 AM when a lump forms at the back of my throat, my chest feels laden with pain, my mouth still tastes of your kiss and reeks of those terrible last words. I just scrolled through my contacts thinking I could talk to someone I haven't spoken to in a while, thinking it will be good to finally take my mind off of you. It was only after I was left with no names and a tear drop that I realised there's no one else I know, who knows me like you do. You're the only person to offer me both destruction and comfort. I don't need you but I do. This is when I feel the most alone. I wonder about the ones that might be awake with me at this time. Do they feel this broken too? Maybe I'm not alone, after all. I wonder if you are just as restless. Does it bother you? All the other nights after 2, we'd be all over each other, our bodies thrown together like they belonged that way, but not tonight. I guess I'll stay awake and visit the beginning, all over again. I guess this is why relationships end. When they want to fix it but they are too hurt to initiate an apology. When they are secretly hoping for a call that never really comes. This is going to be a long night.

I am
Sorry

15.

Tonight is wishful, tonight is kind. For once, it isn't smothering my dreams. For once, I'm smiling without anyone having to make me. You're away but I'm not lonely. It's different. I'm breathless, reckless. You can't bring me down. No one can. Nothing seems to matter. I'm in the beyond. I am forgetting your disdainful kisses and beginning to taste freedom. It's beautiful. Tonight, I belong to myself and for once, I am enough.

16.

You and I
On the brink of separation
In the midst of rumination
Each breath pricks like needle
To think you touch only my skin
But feel everything underneath
Your fingertips dip in my bloodstream
I feel your warmth
Flow through me once again
What went wrong?
You're walking away
I don't want to move, not yet
My eyes refuse to stop memorising
Your form, your ways
Which moments from now
They will not see
To think this is the last time
We will ever be us
Pause, let this moment last
Longer than it was meant to
Stay, for two more minutes
Maybe don't leave at all

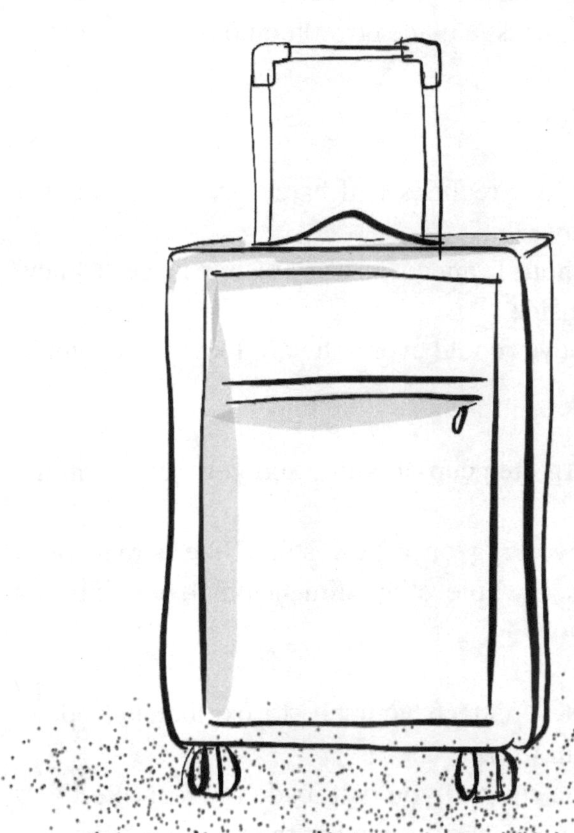

17.

The day after you left, I saw you at our place —
Well, it's just a place now. I could not bear to look
at you, not yet.
You were still

You to me, our realities had barely even separated. I
wasn't ready.
But the minute I landed in front of our place, I knew
you were inside
Before my eyes could even see you. I knew you would
be

alone. A forgotten cup of coffee and your laptop on the
table.
You'd be working on a new story, like a man on a
mission, in a whole other dimension. It was always
easier for you

To completely detach yourself, to explore untrodden
trails of your mind.
It wasn't the sight of you that made me feel like I was
disintegrating by the minute but the fact that I knew

Exactly what must have been going through your mind
Just by the way your index finger had been resting upon
your bottom lip.

It is a privilege to know somebody like that when you're with them. But it is the most tormenting feeling when they are

Long gone and you find yourself on the outside, with the knowledge of their ways still residing within you. You don't know what to do with it anymore.

I took a long look at you hoping it to be the last one and quickly walked away before you could step out of the door to light your cigarette.
I hated that I knew that. I hope to forget soon.

18.

Afraid, cautious, calculating
You fill most of my days
With your ways
Oblivious, unheeding, not knowing
I am enamoured of you
And I misconstrue
Every gesture, every word
Even the ones unheard
Hopeful, naive, beaming
You speak of expectations
From your tomorrows
But I am already there
Spending countless Januaries to Decembers
Cosy by a fireplace with dying embers
Keeping each other warm
There, you kiss me out of habit
But it doesn't mean any less
There, we make love in candlelight
Our bodies are seamless
Aloof, foolish, unbelieving
Today, you are by my side
Yet seemingly distant
You are closer to me in a future
Which is reminiscent
Of a great love
Patient, persistent, wishing

Maybe you will feel tomorrow
The way I feel today

19.

Sometimes I wonder if you changed the scent of my skin just by touching it for as long as you did. My manner of speaking must have become like yours over the years somehow and

Now I can't even tell them apart. Parts of you were so deeply integrated with mine. Do you remember? Our days used to have the same storyline. Sometimes, even today, when my hair brushes against my shoulder

It's a lazy afternoon again; your breath is on me and your kiss is about to rest

On the nape of my neck.
I wonder if we slowly become the people we love

Today I look above
And see clouds turn into objects just the way you did. The hallways of my heart still echo your footsteps. It remains the most familiar sound.

Maybe that's how it goes.
I used to be myself once. Now, I am just a remnant of you.

stories of
YOU &
STORIES of me

20.

I used to love winter once, now I find it to be ruthless. It freezes flowers, just as it freezes time. The sky is always without the caramel sunshine. Now I am edgy during the season, afraid I'll be cold to never recover, to never be warm again. I cover myself from head to toe with layers, and with thoughts which aren't of you and stay indoors when I can; because the touch of the icy wind feels like your fingers against my skin again, sending chills down my spine. Because being with you was akin to being locked up in a morgue with a loved one long gone. Winter is a brutal reminder of the ghastliness, of the suffocation of once belonging to you, without even wanting to. Maybe a few years down the line, I won't shudder. Maybe it won't always stay a metaphor. Only not this year, not this time.

21.

I'm fighting to escape my ripples,
You're bound by your own,
But we belong to the same vast ocean,
The same reality that we've known.
You'll see that after sometime,
Stronger tides will stir us incessantly,
Until we aren't where we used to be.
Our paths will align or you'll pass me by;
Either way, for a brief moment,
You'll almost be mine.

22.

I wonder how many lovers
look at the moon and wince.
I wonder how many yearn for things lost, and for
things that are yet to become.
I wonder if it still reminds you of me, the moon.
I looked at it and thought of you. It broke my heart a
little. I have been wondering since.

Maybe if we looked at the moon at the same time, our
eyes could meet again.

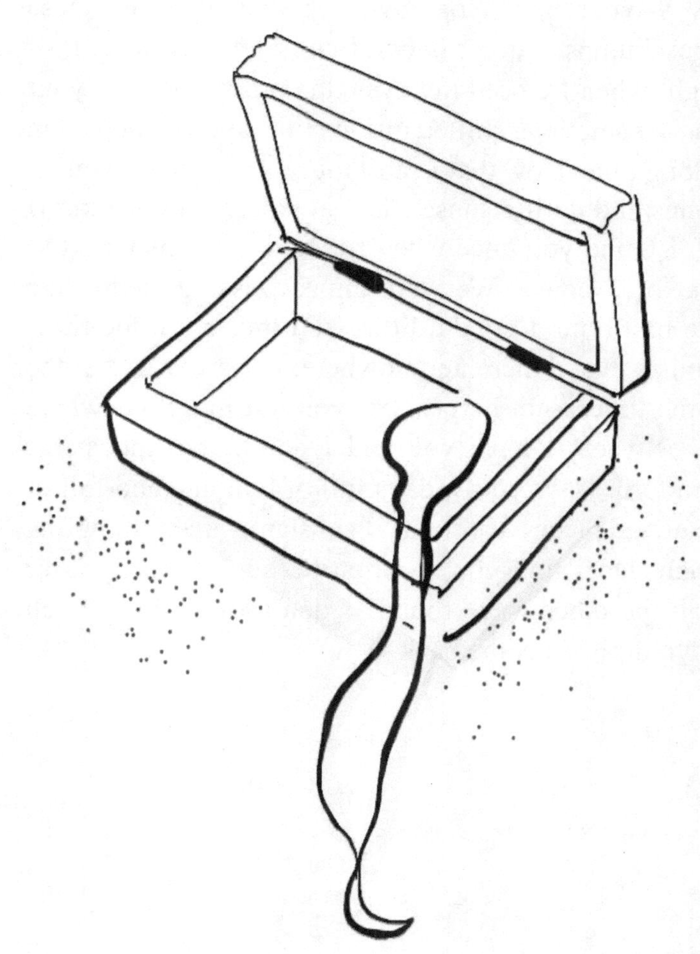

23.

Was it the wind that grazed against my skin, or your breath on my neck that gave me these goosebumps, I don't know. I can't tell anymore. Last night when I closed my eyes, the pillow felt like your chest, something shifted inside mine, and I slept well in a long time. Now that I can't touch you, I sense you, in songs and during sunsets and at places only we know of. I found you once when I turned the corner next to that blue house. We were almost kissing again, like the first time. I cried a little. You linger. All the time. You're everywhere and nowhere. Far away and at the same time, right here where you left me. Somewhere in between, I have you and I don't. It empties me, I'm torn. Days go by, days full of longing, and full of scattered pieces of you that I constantly keep stumbling upon. Do I find you so often because I miss you or is it the other way around? I don't know. I can't tell anymore. Just come back.

24.

I look down at my own hands and they seem alien to me, without your fingers filling up the spaces between mine. I feel empty in the curves of my waist, the small of my back, the parting of my lips. In all the places you had touched me, you are etched. My skin had been like sand, perhaps, that now I'm marked from head to toe in your footprints. Like mountains without valleys or like a lone piece of a puzzle, I can't seem to make sense without you. I miss you in all of my hollows. So much so, that slowly, I'm becoming a void, entirely. But that's a good thing, I guess. Maybe as a void, I'll feel whole once more.

Our Jigsaw Puzzle

25.

You're the tectonic shift that changed my design, the tremors I still feel in my bones. You're the deep scar on my face, the indelible stain on my fabric. You're the phantom pain that keeps me wincing days after the hurt is gone. Sometimes I run into you in my own reflection and sometimes, when I take a walk down an untrodden path alone, I meet you in my shadow. Perhaps when I had you, I shed my own skin and wore yours, that now I'm always dressed in your memories. Perhaps our molecules mingled when we collided, that now I'm made up of you, entirely, and you don't escape the things you become.

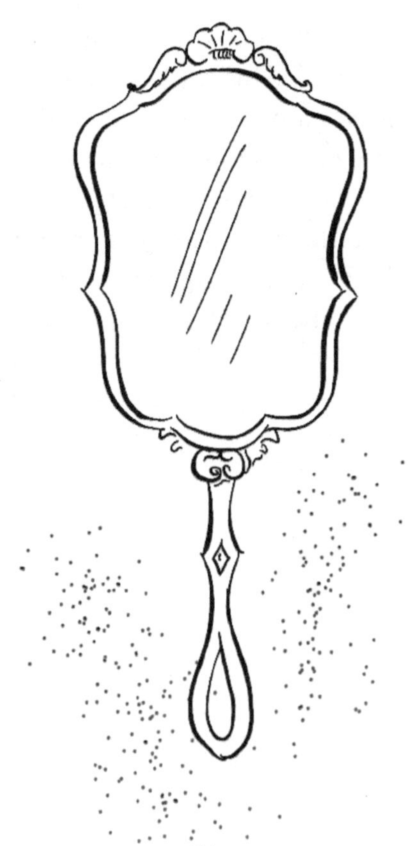

26.

The sun sets upon my lids
   it's night behind closed eyes
the moonlit trail leads to
wherever you are
and I'm with you again
split in half
i'm in two places at once
yet it only hurts here.

27.

And then I thought
maybe love was like the sunlight
I could try and capture the rays
with my bare palms and fail
or I could stand still and bask in it
let it warm me with its molten touch
then let it leave when it's time
have a little faith and see it
come back to me
day after day
and maybe when liberated
it would stay mine.

28.

Inside my heart are a hundred alleyways
paths walked by everyone I've ever met and faint
imprints of everything that I've ever kept close.
They have stains from all the sweet sweat of lovemaking
and from all the tears that I could not stop from pouring,
after several glasses of wine.
They have flowers that bloomed through the cemented
grounds and the creepers that still grow around my
windows.
And on a lonesome night alone
I take a walk down one of these
and every step is a sharp pain in the abandoned cavities
and the further I go, the more I'm haunted
by screeching sounds of unfinished stories and of
unforgotten memories.
Some memories are palpable even now and sometimes
when the sky roars, the smell of rain is your scent.
Now when I scream into the empty halls
the echo of my voice doesn't quite sound like my own.
Maybe I'm losing my mind
and my insanity is rooted in everything that I've ever
lost
like a beloved crayon, a delicate dress
the last sliver of hope when you left, and most of all
the pieces of me that you took along.

29.

If I sent you a postcard
with glimpses of my hours spent without you
would you smile?
would my handwriting warm your heart again
the familiar cursive that used to tell you what my
voice couldn't
do you think you can still understand why I picked a
black pen over blue
or why I still think about you
my estranged lover
in a city so far away
that what I've left behind
can't even reach me
but sometimes the wind sings songs from our lost time
and my eyes find you in foreign faces
and I want to say hello
it's been a while
are you fine? do you miss me?
my world remembers what I try to forget
and makes me wonder
that after all this time
if I sent you a postcard
my darling
would you finally ask me to return home?

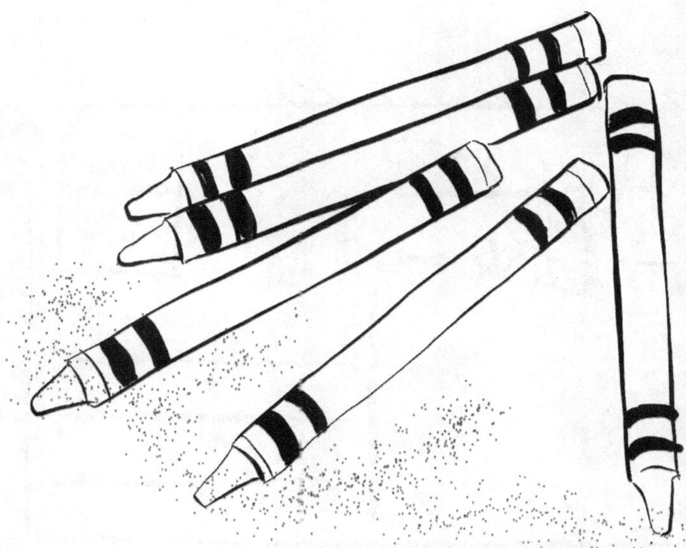

POST CARD
PLACE ONE CENT STAMP HERE

30.

I've been running away
from my worn out tapestry and tarnished heart
my own reflection screams back at me
with words that corrode my strength
and take me straightaway to the forgotten graveyard
where every night is moonless
then I run all the more
breathless as I collapse on the ground
I have nowhere to go
nowhere to hide from myself
I'm always within my reach
even a stranger on the road seems more familiar
than this face that I wear all the time
one that you recognise and I don't
your fingerprints still remain on my cheeks
from all the tear stains that you once wiped
where were you though
when I was trembling in my bed
losing threads from my fabric
weeping, wincing, withering
you ran away
and now I must do the same
until I can look into a mirror
without running into you.

31.

When did love become so desirable yet unattainable? It must have been real at some point. Perhaps when feelings were simple but times were not. Tucked in the crack of war, in the arms of precariousness, the only way to live was in the moment. Loss was like a clingy neighbour knocking at the door. And the only way to have something at all was to give it your everything. There was profound honesty that was found in love, even in the midst of grime and deceit and murder. Perhaps love was nothing but the grappling fear of losing that, at the drop of a bomb. It made you brave. Now? Life is much simpler and feelings, not so much. The clock ticks in reverse and hearts grow empty. That's why it gets so difficult to find. Perhaps it's a concoction only a catastrophe can stir, and perhaps love, real love, can only bloom in tragedy.

32.

You said my strong was delicate, the kind you'd put your faith into but would also want to hold and heal.

I said I didn't believe that, I said I was weak. I bared my bruises to push you away and you stroked them.

Your eyes gleamed at the blues and the blacks and the greens and you said I was art. Not a landscape but abstract, the kind the artist puts his life into creating. Awed by many, understood by few. I said I was nothing but a small, insignificant speck of dust.

I revealed my ugly to push you away and you said I was beautiful.

I don't see it, I said. You don't see what I see, you said. I see you, and everything after you will always be tainted by that. You say that now, I said, but this won't last. Maybe forever isn't about a lifetime, you said. Maybe it's about the extent of time that you don't get enough of and maybe I've just lived one with you. Then just stay, I said. You didn't say a word.

33.

I'm always scared. So scared. That I'll drive you into a conversation with another girl, and tucked in the wee hours of nighttime, it'll have more meaning than our first one ever did, and that suddenly, you'll start preferring her scent to mine. It'll be her words crafting tales and you'll be watching her lips move in awe, tasting kisses that are yet to happen.

And one day I'll call you and you'll let it ring through, your mind impatiently waiting for my name to disappear and her chat window to light up your screen again.

Her silly jokes will make you laugh and everything that we've ever shared will become vile. I'm so scared of the time when this thrill will fade out, it will - it always does, it always has. They have all grown tired, I've seen it in their weary smiles. I'd never known hours could feel so heavy, until I had to bear the weight of a dying almost.

Somewhere between falling asleep and waking up, when the sky transitions, something has always shifted and suddenly, they've woken up not feeling the same way.

When two people end something, both of them feel their hearts break but somehow I'm always on the more painful end. I've always been.

And here you are telling me that it won't happen with you. I want to believe you, I really do but I don't know

if I can. Maybe if we manage to get past the beginning, and I still find you here, telling me the same things, looking at me the same way you did the first time we met. Maybe if I feel enough, for once, to you.
Oh I'll believe and I'll hold your hand into old age, when our faces distort but our familiar eyes still love, and your mouth has swallowed all of my fears. I'll believe you eventually, if you're willing to make me. But I'll understand if you grow tired on your way. Because right now you're saying hello, but all I'm hearing is a goodbye.

34.

When I'm home alone, I often find myself staring at the door, in anticipation of a soft knock or the doorbell ringing or even a phone call that says, "open the door, I'm here." I frown and I look for answers.

Is it because once on a frightful night even the sound of thunder couldn't eclipse the raging voices of my parents fighting and my mom had left banging the door shut so loud that the crackling of a storm went by unnoticed? I hadn't seen her for days. That sound had haunted me for years.

Is it because once I had come through a door only to see my grandma dying right in front of my eyes? That door had brought silence that still comes and goes.

You had left 2 hours ago after a fight yesterday, and time hasn't moved still. I'm frozen. Waiting. Just the loud thud of the door and then the pounding of my heart. Why aren't you back yet?

Doors have never been synonymous with arrivals but always with leaving. And I'm always the one who is left. Inside. Trapped by my own past and my own fears, in knots that I keep fighting, in ropes that keep slicing through my flesh, hurting me.

So I stare at the door again, in anticipation of some kind of an arrival, one that will set me free but also one that never really comes.

35.

You see my 2 pm mulberry smile
distracted, the act of pretence that washes over
my shores from high tides
not my 4 am swollen eyes that don't close
from the sound of my heart pounding
like the branch against my window, of the willow tree
right outside
you see my mind as I show you,
completely wary of where it wanders off to, on most
nights
like it's sleepwalking and the door was left opened
it gets really dark in here, unguarded and unsafe
whatever spills, overflows
and floods over everything I've known
you see my strength, the residue that remains from old
battles
not the pulsating fears that I bathe in every time I shower

so you tell me that you love me

but if my tears don't feel like blood oozing out of a
wound on your skin, and if my pain lets you breathe
if an argument doesn't seem futile and isn't interrupted
with a kiss
if your ego constructs a wall and jealousy paints it the
colour green

if it's always more about you and less about me
you don't love me
so please don't say you do

love isn't just balmy wind and palm trees
it's a winding road in a thunderstorm

it nurtures, it stays
it doesn't watch you like you're a ticking time bomb
it isn't just romance and laughter
it's respect and compromise,
changing for the better
it doesn't hold you hostage,
but it's like a badge you wear everywhere that you go
it isn't a roadside milestone to cover
but the entire journey that remains

loving me is like being in a war zone, I know that
there's no guarantee that you'll ever return home safe
but if you knew all of me, staying would also be hard

so don't tell me you love me
because I will believe you.

36.

I like to read about everything. Sometimes I just sit with my browser open and throw strange questions into the vast space of the Internet, and get answers. It's comforting to know things.

My parents often tell me stories of how I'd always look at things with a sense of wonderment and how my favourite thing to ever ask was, "why?" They'd get annoyed sometimes, they'd really feel proud the other times. So they'd get me encyclopaedias to find my answers in. I loved answers.

I once read that humans shed the upper layer of their skin every two weeks. That's how scars fade and wounds heal. So your kiss has already been erased from my lips and my body has forgotten your touch. That's relieving.

But then I also read that some cells don't renew at all. That's how our skin wrinkles and ages. What if you left an impression on those very spots, and all that you ever made me feel will only grow with me? Because I still remember. More vividly as days pass by. That's terrifying.

Memories blur with time. The mind weakens with age.

But somehow, it always finds a way to remember what our skin may forget. That's strange.

I wish I was a brand new person, one that had never met you. But you see, that's not possible. Some part of you has mingled with some part of me in a way that it will never detach. Why? I still don't know the answer to this one. Sometimes, that bothers me but sometimes that's comforting too, you know. Not knowing.

37.

We were paper boats in a puddle
     so delicate, a brisk breeze away
from spinning in separate directions.
so transitory, a season away
from being thrown into a purposeless corner
where all forgotten things go.
yet, we tumbled together in motion
round and round we went
orbiting around what we thought was love
amused and innocent
awaiting storms so we could last
in the little world that was overcast
and when the sun came
we had nowhere to be
now I wait for another rainstorm
to bring you back to me.

38.

"I love you to death", you'd said.
my finger had shushed you then. it's hard to imagine a life without a habit.
wake up, brush your teeth, shower, dress up, go to work, eat, sleep. stuck in a routine.
our kisses had been caught up in them too.

yesterday, when I hurried out the door for my meeting, you were on the porch reading the newspaper, doing your regular crossword and I gave you an obligatory kiss before getting into the car. It barely lasted a second, a fleeting peck worth forgetting.

later that day when my phone blared with the news of you gone, I thought of the last moment and I could barely remember the details.

I always used to say, "every kiss of ours would be short enough to allow you breath, but long enough to leave you short of it." then how come, I had forgotten my own words?

"I love you to death", you'd said but I had always pushed that thought for a day that would hopefully never arrive.
now that it was here, I didn't know how to survive.

you were gone, and gone was every chance to kiss you, hold you and to tell you, "I love you to your death, and in the unrequited years that will follow, until my very last breath, until we meet again tomorrow."

THE TIMES
YOU & ME

39.

You spoke of weekend getaways
	but I had already been travelling
through your mind
seeing this holocaust of a world
transform into a newfound highland
a fantastical masterpiece
of a miniaturist
who had been crafting
our lives the way we'd pictured it
one intricate detail at a time
we were so happy there
untouched by problems
under a dome made of glass
our very own place

and I didn't know just how much
comfort could mean
until you held me there
and I let go of myself
like cloudburst
it felt like the silence that falls
after the wailing sirens fade into distance
the relief you feel
on a Saturday night about Sunday

winter wasn't cruel anymore
but magical
any where wasn't too faraway
it was the perfect illusion
an infinity
within the see-through walls
of a sky made of glass
and the glass made of memories
and memories made
of all the moments that we made

just you and I
inside a snow globe
tasting freedom and
snowflakes
orbiting around our favourite love songs
cuddled up in sweaters knitted with our stories
on a bed made of love
where we fell asleep
and woke up to a
weekend
every single day.

40.

It's marvellous how
one finds their way to the one
they belong with
sometimes, it's a journey across
countries
sometimes, even the stars
have to align a certain way
and sometimes, you're sitting there
right across from them
the Universe watching in anticipation
two people so perfect for each other
be this close and never meet.

41.

It took an entire candle
to melt on my skin
the hot wax dripping
spreading, then breeding

to understand
your carnal desires
to notice the barb wires
around your wayward heart
keeping me out in the dark
cold, shivering, then derailing
losing control over my own heart

my heart
that didn't know of schemes
and games and perverse acts
but only knew how to love

my heart, like creepers
growing upon other things
holding onto you and falling deeper
so not to fall apart
and you
using it as an ornament
an accessory to dispose off
once you've had enough

it took my burning skin
and peeling of old scales
to finally grow my own roots
deep enough to rely on
it hurt like knives carving
freedom on my arm
but I swear
it felt like freedom too.

42.

like the sky is always there but i only notice it sometimes. and it's during those times, that i can't stop staring.

you were there. then you were not. i could've let you stay, but i couldn't think as clearly back then. fear grappled my senses so firmly, the scars still burn sometimes.

they say that time heals everything but this wound that you've left me with only deepens, darkens. and this pain that used to seem unbearable once is the only thing that makes me feel alive now. it's the only way i can still feel you around. and without it, without you, i don't make much sense to myself anymore.

i don't miss you like sunsets or even moonlit nights. your absence is more like the sighting of a rainbow or a shooting star, or even a comet passing by. fleeting but so impactful, my body still gets tremors from that day.

i miss you more, in emptiness, when i'm alone for it resembles the state of my heart.

before you were gone, i only knew to miss for days or months, then to forget the feeling. i had not once missed anyone with this permanence of time. the kind of missing that's futile. the kind that only comes with an eternal loss, death. the kind that came with losing you.

i miss you like that all the time. i wish there was an escape but i wish for a lot of things and mostly, i wish to go back in time, to the day i couldn't even look at you without flinching, and hold you instead, until you really have to go.

maybe then, it won't hurt as much, missing you.

43.

I opened my eyes
and in five heartbeats
worth of time
you told me
I was no more your muse.
it took me five minutes
to understand
that our clustered yesterdays
would be torn apart
ruthlessly now, in a haste
for you to leave
on a plane
to a multi-verse
that I don't exist in.
"I'm sorry about this"
you said
with your eyes
elsewhere
entry denied
and I sat on the sheet
we made love upon
night after night
with a broken heart
and five empty words
scattered like a
jigsaw puzzle

with missing pieces.
I didn't cry
there wasn't going to be
enough tears
to mourn after
the five years
we spent
drawn upon each other
with stencils
in permanent marker.
now my days are darker
than your tousled black hair
inviting new fingers
to ruffle through it.
It's been five months
since you left
and I'm still
peeling off the glue
that kept us together.
last night
when a thunderstorm
woke me up
I was terrified
that it was you
and it took me
five seconds to realise
you were never here to last
just like the bad weather.

44.

The red in my tired eyes
makes blood look
dull in comparison
the nerves resemble
roots sprouting through
a concrete wall

and there you are
inches away from me
not noticing them at all
so I put on a dreary smile
like a bright shade
of lipstick, to cover up
my bruises and pain
hoping you wipe it
with your fingers
and kiss away the stain

instead you only notice
my smile, and not the quivers
that struggle to hold it
so I put on a show
every morning

and you believe it.

45.

Hot sand burns my feet
so I seek to drown them in rhythmic waves now.
sometimes I walk waist deep
into the sea and stand there
unsteady yet unfaltering.
do you remember how afraid I used to be?
things are so different now. I am so different now.
I wish you could see me, embracing the wilderness of
my heart. I used to think I was made of dunes, now I
take shelter underneath the lush trees I grew with my
own resilience.
they bring rain and cool winds,
sunshine and shade and I, dance with the rustling
leaves, change with time, just like they do
and find beauty within myself in every state.
I'm so whole that I could easily spend a lifetime in my
own company. In unhurried days, in my own unusual
ways.
because I got myself here.
you said I was selfish in doing so but had i not been,
I'd have been miserable in my own skin.

46.

It was like clutching sand
with your fists
he didn't know how to keep me
from running down
so I fell through his crevices
in all the wrong places.

47.

You told me once
that you loved my poems
for their endings
and me
for the reek of last night's
breakdowns and melancholy
when beads of sweat
trickled down my body
you liked to hold me fiercely

you pecked my smiles
but devoured my tear-stained
face
you loved me more
when I was laced
in pain

so I sipped you like my
morning coffee
like you were my cure -
an antidote
that walked in every night
through the door
but left early morning
with no footprints
on my floor

A Garage Sale of Lovelorn Things

and I never wondered why
you ached for me to ache
why you danced to the tunes
of my heartbreak
you visited only on
cloud-cast days
eclipsing me in your
confining embrace

my wounds began to fill
my scars began to fade
I never saw you in the Sun
only in shade

so I wrote you a poem
with a happy ending
and you stared at me
with confounding eyes
your troubled face
my warning sign
to prepare for a hasty goodbye
i cupped your face
in my palms one last time
because darling,
you were never my cure
just a disguise.

48.

We've only ever known ourselves by our own interpretation. and to anyone else in the world, we're fabricated differently. no two eyes see the same person when they see you or me. and the realest life to lead would be one where you're completely, unabashedly yourself. right? although, even then people's understanding of you would widely depend on their understanding of the human world. in a way, we're collectively living so many lives, in so many different sets of eyes.

so it is possible that our paths may have crossed. we could've been at the same café or pub at the same time waiting for different people, or standing right next to each other at a sundowner. we could've been in a queue for popcorn at the same theatre; and during one such a time, a stranger must've seen us — together. their eyes must have captured what we, in the moment, couldn't possibly have recognised. because it wasn't time yet. and I wonder how many times people end up together like that. before, they, quite inevitably, lay their eyes on each other.

49.

It wasn't religion that decided my place of faith. It was subliminal at the time — but a realisation regardless, felt in the moment; like I had been hit by a bolt of lightning. The first shift in my body was because I had looked into your eyes too long. I knew I wasn't in the same place, like realities had been swapped and I had been dealt the best cards. The second shift came like the waves of the sea, and in moonshine we were asked to dance, and we swayed in synchrony, effortlessly. The third and final shift was what aligned all my pieces and put me back together, like I was a Rubik's cube in the hands of a genius. And you, you knew me before I knew myself. I could never understand how you figured out a way to navigate through the minefield that was my heart — but you did, and when our feet firmly rooted themselves in the same soil, I realised, that a place of faith could be anywhere in the world, if found to be in the presence of love.

50.

My grandmother passed away when I was 10 years old. That was the first piece of my heart that I ever lost. The second was when I met you.
It was your eyes that gave away the premonition, and yet I looked into them like a child sneakily staring at an eclipse. I was afraid I'd never see such a spectacular sight. You were a phenomena to occur once in a lifetime.

The summer before she died, my grandmother had been sitting in her chair, on the Veranda of our old house soaking in the morning Sun, and she called out my name. It was almost like she knew, like she had already made up her mind. She looked at me like I was the eclipse and told me, "When you really fall in love, your heart will break a little at the realisation. That's how you know. It's euphoria and pain, and life is never the same." I could never fathom what that meant, but whilst mourning her, I held onto those words like the last pieces of her and never really let go. 15 years later, in your nearness, I fully understood what she'd meant. My life would now be reminisced forever, before and after you.

51.

The night is quiet
without the buzz of your voice
without the mountains and valleys
of your breaths
without your arms reaching for me
on the spread of my bed
without your warm body tingling me whole
without our eyes secretly meeting
in the crevice of midnight
with a shared smile that speaks in soul
without your subconscious kisses
on my spine
without my length draped in yours
like two parallel lines
without you
I'm roads covered in snow
I belong somewhere in your wintry depths
I feel it all the time but in your absence, I know.

52.

There are too many
hours in a day
and too little of me
that remains
I'm candle wax melting
around the sides
of the shape
your fingers gave me
I don't even need
to burn to hurt
It is who I am now
It is how I'll cease to be.

53.

Ever since you left, my soul has aged deeply. It has also yearned for you deeply. The feeling remains like a dull ache in my chest, never allowing my heart to rest.

Funny, how when I had you, I'd still ache. Maybe the bruises you left me with have stained my fabric so permanently, that I can't even remember myself without it.

I was never happy with you, now I'm not happy without. So nothing has changed really and yet, everything has. My heart beats to the pace of your footsteps walking towards my door, then out, slamming it on my face. It stops briefly then. But the tears don't. It happens over and over again.

My mind has a neon sign hanging on its wall that reads, "I'll never be enough." It is a pulsating headache I wake up with each morning. I'm torn, worn out, yet decorated in guilt.

How did you do it? Make me feel like we were having our tryst when I was only lovelorn. Now I walk on my own, but you still have a hold over my shadow. I was used to getting by with a little help from a bottle of wine and slim cigarettes, but, I'd still yearn for you and hate myself for it.

But tonight, when the darkness seeps in after sunset and I'm filled with remorse - for once, I will not blame myself, or even hate myself. It wasn't my fault that I landed in the hands of a master puppeteer. And maybe if I keep reminding myself of it, I will get over this fear, and finally see it for what it really was. I am no more yours to break, to toy with or to tame. I will have my shadow back, and make you take back, your shame.

54.

I like you in the quiet
while you're asleep
when our differences
and arguments have closed shop
and won't reopen until
11:00 AM
so I ask you to sleep in
for a little bit longer tomorrow
because our bodies
don't understand
why we disagree on so many things
all they crave is touch
so in the hush, I feel the pull
I look at you with your eyes
closed
I've conversations with you
during that time
things I wouldn't say in daylight
and certainly not when awake
no matter the mood
we always find a way
to fall asleep, entangled
free of any discomforting
thoughts
I like you in the quiet
for in silence, I don't find reasons

to push you away
sleep a little longer, love
I find courage to be vulnerable
when you're not looking.

55.

And I wonder sometimes, had I been a book, what I would've been all about. I think I'd be an old one, an early print, with dog ears and coffee rims on my pages. a person's signature coupled with a message to a daughter, a lover, a grandchild, with paragraphs marked and underlined. one with an unkempt, battered cover. I think I'd be a book that has been passed on and on, one that has had a journey. I'd have travelled through many bookshelves and neighboured alongside many great books.

on my worst nights I think, I'd be one that has not once been looked at, in a library.

and on my best, I think if you were ever to browse the dusty bookshelf I'd be on, you'd pick me.

for all the reasons others did not.

56.

It's a scientific fact that because light takes time to reach us, everything we see is in the past. I read that somewhere. Maybe that's why I felt like I'd already met you before, when we'd only just met.

And you said, "I met you at the wrong time." My heart broke before you could even break it. Because there's a clock tower in my soul and I've had conversations with it. It's told me that there's no such thing as the "right time", and if at all there was, it'd be the Planck time it took for anyone to realise that this person could be the one that stays. That very moment, in which you feel like a teenager again, with a hopeless crush is the only right time to go forward with it.

Einstein said that for physicists, the distinction between the past, present and future is only an illusion. So to think, there'd come a day when life won't be as chaotic, work not as needy, and heart not so frightened to take that leap of faith, we're only fooling ourselves. I wish I could tell you that. But you've made up your mind, and I, I'm too tired to waste a breath on somebody who doesn't already know this.

I wish time wouldn't pass slower, the faster we moved. Because with every second that progresses, I fall in love a little more, a lot faster, and that means it'd take only that much longer to move on.

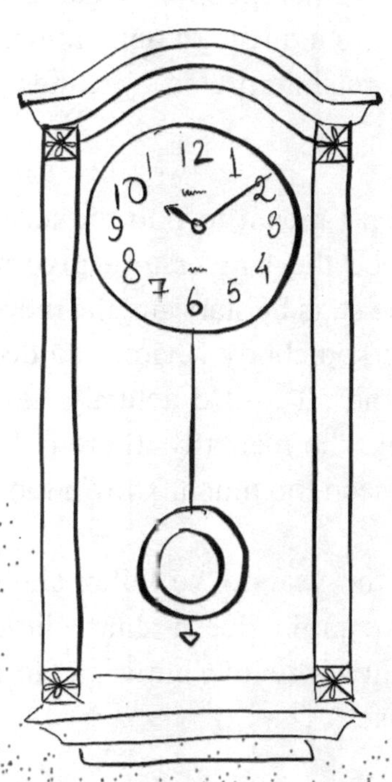

57.

1. what's the past if not a bunch of stories people have shared with other people. a game of Chinese Whispers, spoken to a queue of generations, often lost in translation, or misinterpreted by minds of different wavelengths.

2. I think we aren't meant to find the answers to our existence. to probe the Universe to give us answers. because if I let the stars be stars and the moon be moon, if I let myself be somebody I hadn't so deeply gotten to know, flaws and all — I'd actually have a shot at happiness. I think, the mentally ill are only depressed because they've seen too much, known too much.

3. what if, over the years, I've fallen slightly in love with pain. because until it doesn't hurt a little, it doesn't seem real. and that's why love hurts. and loss hurts. and wounds and bruises.

4. I often find myself thinking of death for it feels like a real possibility now. I almost never think of mine, but anyone who has a piece of me — my parents, close friends, pets, I look at them and break down. Is this what they mean by loving somebody like you're going to lose them?

5. last night, I ordered dinner and immediately put in the fridge. there are a lot of meals in there, from this week and even last, and I hate myself for not having the appetite but the privilege still, to waste food when there's so much poverty, in such close proximity. yet I'm helpless, feeding myself with lies instead, sleeping in a bubble.

6. I stay up until mornings these days because I've trouble sleeping alone. somehow mornings seem a lot friendlier than nights.

7. if I wrote about you enough, could I then at least conjure up your shadow? or better, could there be a chance that you'd read them and let go of all the worldly, futile, imaginary boulders that've been keeping us apart?

58.

1. Ironically, the open sky is a ravel of mysteries. Yet all we see when we look above is uninhibited vastness, which seems to us like freedom from where we stand.

2. And in that open space, there are a billion things unknown to us, and so unknown to themselves. Because so far, only humans have been able to decipher any meaning from the Universe and beyond. At least that's what we like to think. But have we deciphered anything at all?

3. Sometimes I think, the only things that are genuine are ones that still remain inexplicable to us. Things that even our brilliant minds can not articulate with their sound logic and reasoning. Things that often leave us feeling helpless because we cannot control or define them.

4. I'm far from knowledgeable when it comes to physics and the comprehension of the cosmos but I am a poet, who finds inspiration in the stars. And I see there is a pattern that surrounds us, if you really look. Scientists will give it a name, mathematicians will have something else to add but to me, it's a grand design, a piece of art and we are mere fragments of it.

5. Earlier today, I read about binary stars. They are two stars that are gravitationally bound together, orbiting their common center of mass; and I immediately ran out to spot them. It's the rarest sight, impossible to see even through the most powerful telescope because from this great, great distance, they appear as one.

6. And suddenly to me, that phenomenon became the very definition of love.

7. I'm going to bed thinking that maybe, from a great, great distance, you and I look like binary stars.

59.

I built a house of cards once and heaved that sigh I'd been saving for the final glimpse of what lay before me — and just then, it all fell apart. before I could reach for the camera. before I could savour it for a little bit longer. within the time it takes to blink once. and I wondered if hours of laboured dedication had been worth that one moment of fleeting satisfaction.

we built a relationship, and you wonder why I'm still holding my breath.

A
K
10
7
A
K
Q
7

60.

Tucked under the covers
  you whispered
'but you'll always have me'
wiping my tears away, you said
'you'll make it through the years, you'll see.'
it was all okay until I realised
I couldn't hug a memory.

61.

Compartmentalise, they say.
like everything else in your house has its place, so should every experience and memory. I think the starkest difference between childhood and being an adult has been to discover the grey area. the best way to learn how to swim is to be thrown into the depth of a pool, my father said. probably because he knew somewhere in his heart that life would ultimately do that to me anyway. drown me in the deep, deep ocean of grey I'd only be unfamiliar to. and I'd have to learn to hold my breath until I surfaced and finally saw land.
what's right and what's wrong?
a mistake doesn't define a person. logic and practicality are out to murder the surreal things.
nothing is simple anymore.
opinions. so many opinions.
sometimes I wish I didn't have any, or at least these many. I wish that for other people too.
boxes. so many boxes in my mind.
I've put you in one of them and I haven't used a permanent marker to label anything. I don't want to know where you are, but most importantly, I don't want to kill the possibility of running into you someday. the state of my mind is that of an emptied apartment — the only problem?
I don't know if I'm moving in or moving out,

or if I'm stuck in a time warp, unsettled forever. compartmentalise, they say. but what if there are too many boxes and not enough room to unpack? maybe I'm meant to be this way, always in a frenzy to be somewhere else, never knowing how to stay in the present. right here.

62.

You showed me
I was broken like jigsaw
And not like glass

Without even realising

So when you disappeared that last time
Only to have me aching for you

I did better than to offer you my
Quivering lips with your morning coffee

So you could taste the earthquake

I put my pieces together and became
A morning, without calamity
A night without tremors

And you were a thrill chaser
Without the adrenaline
Needing
More
For the first time

63.

I wrote about love so often that you thought I'd be a rug next to a fireplace on a rain-kissed day, that you could return home to.

you told me my lips were love letters written in quilled ink on aged paper, tucked in a crimson seal.

that I smelled of childhood pinky promises, of seamless forevers and puppy love.

you said my eyes held the horizon where stars and poetry had brief encounters, and the warmth emitted from their rendezvous was the rising of the Sun.

my demeanour reminded you of a quaint stroll along the Seine in Paris and my voice sounded like a string quartet playing in the background.

and I, I told you a whirlwind romance was a wish from the past. that unlike braving the seasons that come and go, I couldn't do the same with love and all the heartbreak it had brought.

now I was rusty and dented from collisions, unable to even feel a spark, like all the electricity in my body had gone out.

I warned you that my temperament resembled the English weather, that you couldn't ever visit without preparing for rain.

but you only smiled and listened like none of it had made a difference and I stood there in disbelief. I hadn't managed to push you away, and despite my utter sense of numbness, I could sense a familiar feeling crawl under my skin.

maybe now, it wasn't about knowing from the very beginning but realising it along the way, that even though I felt vacant then didn't mean I always would, that you would be someone I'd want to love; and to simply have that desire was enough.

64.

My first warning sign
should've been that you
loathed Bukowski's edge
and rawness
I read you one of his poems
one of my favourites, a few lines
you spurned it
and just how long did it take you
to realise that the tongue I kissed with
could also slit throats
with equally remarkable passion?
I think my choices scared you
gave you a glimpse
of doomsday rubbing
its palms together
plotting the end for some
the beginning to others
if only you'd decided to stay
instead of chasing more
saturated gardens
if only you'd watered our
own backyard together
bringing it to life
instead of running away
like a bee caught drinking
nectar, you could've tasted mine.

I had always been love
roughed around the edges
from the rust that came with
too many abandoning
and not enough staying.
but you couldn't be around me
long enough
to figure it out.

65.

The sky bled upon me
it became the ink
I wrote you
poems with

in the process
I became hollow
like the stars
I wrote about so often

I was a poet
with beautiful words
but to myself
I was a dying wish

so I let my soul go
to visit you
one night
it hasn't returned since.

66.

The human heart
beats 115,000 a day
when excited it can double
but when it breaks
it loses count
and numbers do not have
any significance anymcre
So all I have now
are primitive, wild
heightened sensations of pain
and a few stale words
to describe them.

67.

You wreaked havoc
  then covered it up
with an 'I love you'
like we so often did
with our pile of dirty laundry
to forget about it.
a white mountain
with chaos underneath,
bound to avalanche.
no, love wasn't enough
I said
because your love was
an empty bar on a weekday
and that kind never feels like home.
real love is much like
a pile of fresh laundry
made of neat layers of kindness
and care and respect and trust and faith and lust
and friendship and affection and
it keeps growing and growing
like a plant that gets nourishment
and you could never keep a plant alive
even if you tried
no, love wasn't enough
if you didn't even know what it was
your love was a neon sign

hanging outside a store
misleading
and I walked into possession.
the gate closed behind me, the gate had bars.
you tried so hard to tie me up
in ropes
they ask me about marks on my wrist
and I say, it's from a mistake
I wore once.
you built me a fortress
made out of a red cloth
pulled away from a pole
but in that fortress I could still
hear red sirens
warning signs, see the red flags
because at the time, I used to think
that love would be enough
not anymore, no
the fairytales are lies
you were raised like a boy
but I was raised as human.
you lived a fantasy — an archaic fantasy
from centuries ago
so I decided to let go
and you said 'i love you'
but never enough to treat me
like I'm loved
so I decided
that love wasn't enough.

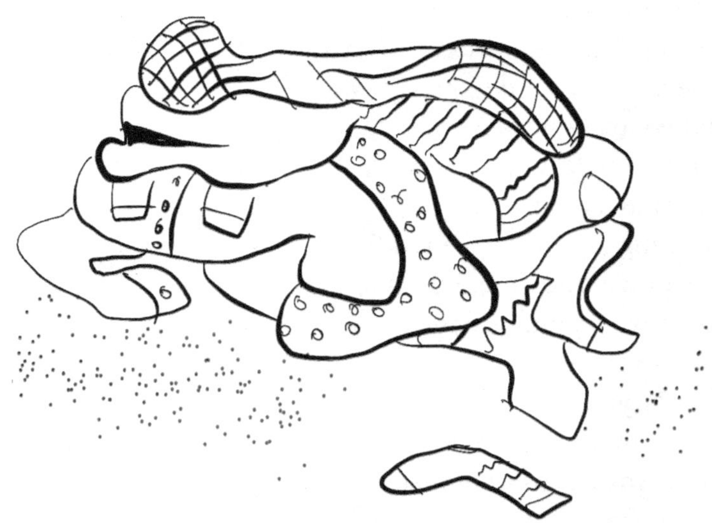

68.

I had a friend who had been fighting a drug addiction. he would tell me his stories of withdrawal and I'd hear them with disbelief, knowing with staunch faith, I'd never have to live through that.

how could separating from something that was so bad for you hurt so much? cause you immediate misery, so much misery, that returning to that bad thing seemed like the only comforting choice?

the first time we kissed, I already wanted to kiss you again. love leapt out of my heart at every sighting of you much like a cuckoo clock and all of my life got tied up to yours like the earphones in my handbag. it was so easy to be yours. until it was hard, then, I was the addict, aware of everything and yet, unable to let go. fitting in words on the last page of my notebook, my handwriting growing smaller and smaller, scribbling, squinting, refusing to turn to a new one.

and I understood how separating from something that was so bad for me could hurt so much, cause immediate misery, so much misery, that returning to that bad thing seemed like the only comforting choice.

my friend overdosed and passed away a few years ago. he couldn't make it.

but I could still break free. and I remembered how on his good days, he used to say, "what's easy now will be hard later and what's hard is hard only for now."

I spent most of last night untangling both our lives while you cried poison and pleaded and begged. your fingers still trying so desperately to control my mind. your eyes, soulless, demented. but I still had my soul. and I had to protect what was left of it. so I ran away, untethered from you.
today is my first day of withdrawal.

69.

I could feel the ground shiver
or was it every inch of me
that trembled
but I swear, when we parted ways
the earth itself split in half
kind of like my heart.

70.

This is where we held hands for the first time. the tantalising heavy breaths we heaved. the tightening grip of fingers, refusing to let go despite the clammy palms.
we didn't let go for as long as we could.

the other day, I tried to slip my hand into yours while crossing the road, out of habit, and your fingers barely wrapped around it. you put it in your pocket as soon as we reached the curb and I knew in that moment, we'd never hold hands like that first time again. or kiss like that first kiss and hug like that first hug.

it was as if the weather had changed in a matter of minutes. it was cold, harsh, brittle. and in the time i took to reminisce that feeling one last time before i'd desperately try to forget it, you, my love... you had already forgotten about me.

71.

Two months ago, I could write to you
In special ink, the kind I only use to write to
Somebody who wants to see me, really see me.

It's the kind that is invisible to anybody else.

With the quill, I spilled
My quivering emotions, in shivering haste
And you read all of it, spread it across your soul

Just to feel my tremors too

Now those letters are unrecognisable. Torn, crumpled
pieces
Of paper been thrown away. It's almost as if they
weren't valuable once

And I sit here wondering
Just when did human emotions become so disposable?
When did I?

Dear

72.

Imissed you today, while I was with my closest
friends. That's when I knew I was in trouble.
Anybody could fill my mind in aloneness
But only you could, when I was cheerful and busy and
happy

I want to tell you that crowded places are no fun without
your face in front of me; blurring everything else out.

I want to tell you that when I am feeling low, I want
you here
Next to me, simply being and I want to bury my head
in your chest and jut stay there

I want to tell you that I want you

I am seeing you again tomorrow

Who's to say this won't really happen?

The moon is almost full tonight
tomorrow, I could be too.

73.

You were different
     you didn't run
you took small steps away
little by little
you built a distance so great
that by the time I took notice
you were already gone
and I, I was too late.

74.

And while on my way back home
I thought about you, what a waste of a beautiful
mind
a heart set on rewind
refusing to beat in the moment. what a waste of a
conversation
of a rare connection
of endless laughter and smiles.
and what's closeness if you were on the other side of
a wall
was it really intimacy at all?
those goosebumps felt like barbed wires
a story lived by two liars
did it even happen?
and if it was loneliness that had led me into your arms
despite those blaring alarms
I feel even lonelier now.

75.

I didn't realise how broken I was until I was held within another set of arms. The confining kind, the familiar kind. It rang a bell, the church-tower kind. And I realised, I can't be reckless with my heart anymore, even if I tried, the girl I used to be, I have left behind.

76.

You cried in my nightmares
and flowers in the garden
sprouted again

the colours unrecognisable
colours of death
petals as fragile as ashes
stems like rotting corpses
leaves of bony, frail fingers
swaying to lost time

it all seemed fine
until I woke up
to normal colours again

I knew I was without
the lingering reminder
without your graveyard eyes
gazing into my soul
what a shame, what a blunder

to fall out of sleep
to feel pain and to weep
and to be heartsick again.

77.

How many leaps of faith
does it take
to run out of hope?
how many
does it take
to get it right?
was it my slight
quivering movement
that caused all the downfalls
was it my slow, deep breaths
or the frantic hyperventilation
was it how quickly
I walked to them
or the slow and hesitant
steps that I took
was it my misguided heart
or was it the world bracing me
for the one final leap
one that tells me
it wasn't me after all.

78.

I tiptoe around you in the dark, so you can't fully grasp my vulnerability. and during the day, I give you a glimpse of only my shadow.
that's how I meet you, in bits and pieces, always
holding back.
because I am always scared
that once you'd have me
you wouldn't want me. I've watched it happen
way too many times, almost as many sunrises I've
witnessed. almost as many sunsets.

79.

You spilled some red wine when we met. and
when you were busy picking up the shards
of your broken glass, that red wine left a bit of a stain
on your tile. It even spilled
into the next morning, I knew the clouds were odd
coloured, on my way back home
after having spent the night at yours.
some of it was on the shirt I'd been wearing, some
dripped on my arm.
the stain was your skin, cold, then suddenly warm
after having touched me.
I have felt warm for days
in the inches around my waist, on my lip, on my nape.
you have cleaned your tile, the weather itself has
changed. clouds are white again.
but I've been avoiding doing laundry. my shirt still
holds the stain. that's how I'm near you.

80.

The river ebbs away
   giving me only
a brief moment
to watch it go
and go
and go.

you were always like the river
almost never still
never mine to have
because that would require staying
and that had never been
your purpose.

81.

You looked into my eyes
like you understood
my deepest shudders
like the branching blue veins
on my wrist
were my tree of life
and I began to look at myself
through your eyes
those vicious little lies

and I thought
if I gave the rain
another name, another sound
another scent
would it become mine?

you laughed at my analogy
while dressing me up
in my nightmares, which were
ironically your dreams
and I had to plead to you
to let me be me

but no matter what you called it
a downpour, a storm, rain
it wouldn't dare change

and it took me a long walk
in dripping clothes
to drop the weight
of your possession
to be clean from
your berating vision
to finally be seen
in the comfort
of my own skin.

82.

The pink skies today reminded me of the tint in your palms, the moment you'd let go off my arms.
I shrugged it off and looked at the big, white moon.
the craters reminded me of bruises long gone, but quite like the moon hiding behind clouds, I could feel their phantom presence.
I shrugged it off and felt the breeze hitting my face and it reminded me of how long it had been since I had felt a touch so gentle that I could compare it to wind.
since I had been loved so endearingly that my chest could heave a sigh as featherweight as the clouds that float by. right now, the word dangles upon my head at a dump-yard — in the midst of cluttered, broken, abandoned things.
be wary, it says. hesitate. scrutinise. nothing good exists. is he for real? look back at your own past and you'll have your answer, it screams at me.
it demeans me and slowly breaks away the clumped clays of hope I'd stolen to hold onto, in times like these. they tell me to write about happier things but I, I've always written from experience and lately, my nights have been more sullen, even darkness refuses to speak to me.

83.

I don't think the night ever ends. and in the a.m.
I find my way back to your doorstep, I pace back
and forth on my tiptoes, I don't want to
wake you. I don't want to break
my dream which is even more fragile than a dandelion
swaying to the wind.
and in the a.m.
I think about quantum entanglement, I don't think
they can mention you without
referring to me. like an antonym.
even though we've got cigarette trailed roads that go
for miles, between us. even though you'd rather burn
your tongue than let my name
rest in your mouth.
even though we dreamed of ending up
in Sicily and now it's off your bucket list.
and our songs are no more
our songs.
all the days arrive with resentment,
laden with broken artefacts that
made sense to only two people, centuries ago.
nights are more forgiving.
they have always been, you take your sorry heart and
arrive at my doorstep someday
in the a.m.
and I might just take you back.

Our
Bucketlist

84.

Meet me near the clock tower
in our dreams, in the lost city
that is dark and uninhabitable
I can forget to read time
you can forget to
forget me.

85.

The dream from last night has my eyes draped,
still. like a projector playing it on a white
dangling sheet. it is so real. we are talking over the
phone. talking about things
I've wanted to tell you. things I've assumed you've
wanted to tell me.
my subconscious is yearning for a closure
that will probably never come.
maybe it's best that way but
the mind is a mysterious thing. it makes me dream
very real dreams. we talk for hours, you know?
you tell me you finally went to Japan. you've got a
steady job, I don't remember
if you're dating. the mind remembers what it wants to,
the bits and pieces that it
knows will not hurt. because we are always conscious
about wounds. and I'm still scraping
the scab over the one you left. that deep, deep cut.
it itches sometimes like an alarm clock set to remind
me to think of you.
like I'd need a reason.
we talk about why you disappeared
without a goodbye and in my dream you say, it was
too hard.
you've been writing books that you never intend to
publish. your aloofness is still

frustratingly endearing to me. your eyes come closer
to mine which is funny
because in my dream, we are talking over the phone.
but I'm seeing you.
the brackets of your smile. the tousled curly hair.
you're using your soft voice, one that you'd concocted
just for me.
I wake up missing you. the wound is fresh again.

86.

I fell in love with you in a way
That even metaphors couldn't help describe.
I wanted to write
Ballads to our romance
Free verses to some
Occurrences
That could not possibly be rhymed.
Perhaps write a cinquain about holding hands for the
first time
A limerick or two about that first date
And a sonnet about the surreality of it all
The intervention of fate.
But I was so happy
And happy people don't write poems,
They say
So I sit here now
In present day
Writing a poem about poems and you
And about how we bid our goodbyes
In a haiku.

87.

When the night complains
    Of a dull ache
I become afraid
For its sake
Do I believe in ghosts?
I don't really know
I don't think the spirits
Could ever haunt me
Only your absence
Only your memory.

88.

Your touch caused ripples
  Upon my skin
So one night
I made you touch
The sky
All the darkness
Was stirred
And
Galaxies were brought
To life.

89.

Iwill take my pretence off
Tonight with my make up,
And as i wipe my lipstick off,
I will not wear a smile, and by
The time I get my mascara,
I will already be crying.

Maybe I am somebody
You have conjured up, a collection
Of my memories
Spread across my bed. My
Scars burn and pain is the
Lullaby that puts me to sleep
Once my eyes turn red.
As i undress for a bath, i will also
Shed my skin until i am
All bones and soul, and feel
Everything.

Then i will dissolve into water
And you submerge into my sins.
Let me show you who i really am
From within.

90.

It wasn't that you couldn't love me
that finally broke me. it was
the scathing indifference —
the fact that you didn't feel
anything
at all.

91.

It rained freckles
on my skin
the December downpour
touched me in places
pain lived in
and it took breathing
in cold air
to let go of the burning
deadweights
that had been there
inside my chest
it took drowning
in an untimely, unprecedented
wintry rain
to realise
that love, music and pain
are universal;
and to unravel into raw, human form
then, to sit in the tenderness,
comfortably
is what it is
to truly live.

92.

I want you to know that I will wear your jacket, even
if it reeks
of seven yesterdays
to make something of you be something of mine
for days that you're not around
and I'm lost in time

and I will ask the moon a favour, to lookout for you
when I can't do so myself
she owes me, you know, for hundreds
of nights I've spent facing up, having our balcony
camaraderie, through all of her phases
so she will help

and if at all you decide to take
your favourite jacket away
if your hand decides to
leave mine
if our love doesn't live
to see another day

I will borrow
the darkest fold of the sky
drape myself
in its midnight blue
land a seat right next to the moon
in the hopes to catch a glimpse of you.

93.

My terracotta skin had chipped away, around its curves and edges
until I was bereft of any art or meaning
until I was only a lump of clay.
I had been living since, oblivious to aliveness, a heaving mess, formless
then your lonely hands found my shape, and it took your artistic vision to build me up from scratch into the old, familiar landscape
was it your knowledge of me that resurrected me to life
or did you make me up as an ideal someone you had wanted
either way, I am no more a lump of clay, I'm more of myself in every way
and everyday, you paint me with yet another intrinsic detail
then you wonder if my ceramic heart
could ever be yours to keep
if you ask me, I can't think of anybody else it could belong to.

94.

I keep the curtains drawn so that way, I could be anywhere in the world. my imagination holds my reality's hand in this bedroom, and I teleport.
I sip on macchiato after devouring the best pizza in a roadside café in Italy.
I watch Before Sunrise and walk the cobbled alleyways of Vienna.
every now and then, I slip away to the west village in New York, my emotions as diverse as the crowd there.
so far I've watched the northern lights, jumped off cliffs, hiked at countrysides. I've been everywhere in my mind, a variety of vibrant finds
but each night, after a great new adventure, I clench my fists, I close my eyes shut
and try really, really hard to end up next to you
and every time I end up right where I began, alone lovelorn, as vacant as the other side
of my bed. my eyes puffed up just like your pillows, trying as hard as I can to remember you
but my mattress doesn't dent from your weight anymore, only my heart seems to grow heavier.
the more you fade, the more I persuade
myself to hold onto
what is so clearly not mine anymore.
so I keep my curtains drawn, to try and forget that we belong to the same city but not to each other
I let my mind take me away to someplace new, as long as it's a place that I haven't been with you.

95.

Ihad a dream
a dream with you
and when your fingers
touched me
I shivered
in my wake.

how long could I've held
onto that sleep
a few more hours, I think
but the morning came anyway
and even though
I tried to hold onto that feeling
that feeling of having you around
the dream I had, trickled down
my body, back and skin
like drops of water
changing shape
blending into more
water
until I was a towel-dried drought
bathed in the stench of reality.

96.

Your smile could alter my breathing
instil life in an otherwise lifeless body
i didn't feel like a black hole that a star becomes when
it dies.

i felt happy. like all that rainfall had been worth it for
this one sighting of
a rainbow.
funny thing, my friend told me the other day this fact
about rainbows.
each one of us has a different antisolar point, so nobody
really sees the same rainbow.
and I thought about how
nobody would see you the way I do. especially
not you. I wish I could lend you
my eyes only so you could admire yourself for all that
you were. are.

we were so effortless in the making, like a cool breeze
blowing into your room at nighttime, humbling you
with relief.
I've been reading a lot lately. stories carry me away
from reality. from you. and the state of my heart. we
were quite the story too, you know, before we got
derailed. we used to be
an epic romance
now we remain a cautionary tale.

97.

I am fluent in two languages, yet no combination of words could weave a sentence persuasive enough to change your stubborn mind. "there are things you can control and then things that you can't." my therapist always tells me.
I don't have much control over my own feelings, forget trying to revive yours.
when the morning light falls on your bedroom wall, you don't see my shadow.
I'm no more real to you than the fears that have you in their grasp. I'm contained time in an hourglass, you're fleeting by.
"I love you, though" you tell me, the words are barely a foetus, and you already have one foot out of the door. you can't possibly keep hurting me, simply because I've a greater ability to endure.
I'm not your smoke break, your lullaby before bed, your dreamy wake.
I'm an impaired machine you are too lazy to repair. I'm fading, fluid, forgettable and I know all these words, so many words. I'm fluent in two languages, and you don't even pick up the phone anymore. the words are rotting in the refrigerator. maybe they will soon be forgotten, I'll soon be forgotten, like the trash you forgot to take out the night we met.

DICTIONARY
PICTIONARY
a collection of our words

98.

I've been alone with you
   my heart is light today
we spent three nights and two days
getting to know each other
with words and without
and I expected burnouts
but I'm an Auckland sky, bright as ever
even though I miss you
it is rooted in longing, not in fear
how have I gone so long without you, my dear?
life unravels a little better now
sadness has a tincture of sweetness
how are you my strength
and my weakness?
I love you, with a dip in the ocean
with relief, in bed
on a lazy Sunday afternoon
and this kind of love
the kind that makes you notice
your breaths
it comes with ease
playful tease, cackling laughter
childlike, wholesome, pure
and with traces of honeycomb
your skin is honey
you're warmth, melting
my iciest corners
we belong on postcards and sunny beaches

misty hills and scenic places
I've not written in a week but speaking to you feels like
reciting poetry
and every night we fall asleep between pages of
literature
I'm so happy, deliriously even —
I can hold you, kiss you, touch you
all at leisure
how are you mine?
this doesn't make any sense
but neither did I, without you.

99.

If one day
The sun sets for you
As it rises for me

I will live
With half a smile
Half a soul
Half an existence
For without you
I am almost
Myself
But not quite.

100.

The wires were cold against my skin and unrelenting to my weaknesses. Yet they comforted me, withholding what was left of me. I could see the effervescence of the outside world. Yet I was relieved being distant from the forbidden land. There I was, on the other side
of the fence, miles away from fragility and chaos. On the other side
of the fence, I could remain unscathed, in the reality
that I had crafted for myself.
I was fine. I was safe.

Then you came along, with promises and dreams
and love. An ocean full of love.
You said you would wait on the outside, until I was
ready to swim again.
You said you would stay for as long as it would take,
and I started to breathe again.
Maybe your soul was streaked
with my favourite colour. Maybe your heart beat
in the same manner as mine. Maybe I wouldn't drown
this one time. Maybe. There was so much hope
in this uncertainty. I didn't need the fence anymore.

I wanted to gnaw my way out to you, break free
from the only safe place that was now holding me
captive.
But the wires were cold against my skin and unrelenting

to my weaknesses.
There you were, still waiting.
There I was, trying to escape
a reality all over again.